Bible Series

"What Does it MEAN... ?"

"Questions asked ***Answers offered"

Lee Banta

ISBN 978-0-359-67766-5

Franzetta Hill Edition

What Does it Mean… ?

"The flesh is still with you at death."

To understand that statement, see 1Cor. 15:22 (KJV)

It says:

"As in Adam, all die, even so in Christ, all shall be made alive."

Adam represents *"the flesh"* because God made him physical from the dirt of the ground. The flesh is what our physical bodies are born into.

Christ represents *"the spirit"* because of Jesus' resurrection from the dead. Spirit is what we are "born again" into when we accept Christ.

If a person is in Christ prior to the time of their passing, they are spirit, and are already resurrected to eternal life. They are *"saved"* from death. Even though their body is dead and buried, it is just an empty shell. They have transitioned into the *domain* of eternal life. They are **made alive.**

But if the person is not in Christ prior to the time of their passing, they are still in Adam… still in the flesh.

So when their body is dead and buried, it is not an empty shell. Their soul is still there, buried with their body for eternity. If you are not saved, "<u>the flesh is still with you at death</u>."

What does it mean... ?

Romans 11:6-8, KJV

(Vs. 6) *"And if by grace, then is it no more of works otherwise grace is no more grace. But if it be of works, then it is of no more grace: otherwise, work is no more work.*

It means:

If it is grace, then it is the free gift of God, and not something that we've done.

If it is something that we've done, then it is not God's free gift of grace, because if it was... we wouldn't have to do anything.

Many people have the misunderstanding that they have to do something for God in order to receive blessings from him. In the Old Testament days, before Christ, people sacrificed animals such as lambs, calves, etc... in order to please God. They had to give, in order to receive.

Today people often say:

"You have to give to others so that you can get your blessings."

That might be true for people as we bless each other in life, which is a good thing, but we don't need to do it just to get blessings from God. We should do it from the heart, and let it become part of us. That's how we get blessings from God. Some people are so giving, that they will give you their last. They are willing to sacrifice for the sake of others. Isn't that what God did for us by sacrificing his Son?

If we are believers, we already have God's blessings in the form of his grace. The only sacrifice needed was made by Jesus on the cross, which is why he is called the *"lamb of God."* Our actions of doing something in an effort to get God's blessings is *work*. The only work needed was already done by Jesus.

(Vs. 7) *"What then? Israel hath not obtained that which he seeketh for; but the election hath obtained it, and the rest were blinded."*

It means:

This is what happened. In the Old Testament days, all the people of Israel wanted God's blessing, but not all of them got it. Some of them did because they pleased God with their sacrifices, or the way they worshipped him.

The others became hard and angry because of it, and turned away from him.

Isn't that how it is with people today? We often look at the lives of other people, and see how God has blessed them. Then we become angry, and jealous because he didn't bless *us* in that way. We become judgemental, just like the people of Israel must've become.

No one can know the mind of God, or the reason he blesses some in one way, and others differently. No one knows the criteria that God requires. No one knows the level of the blessing he has prepared for each individual person. No one even knows the timing of it.

In the same way as those Israelites, many people become hard towards God, and turn away. They develop an *"Oh well"* type of attitude, losing faith. Some people think they can take matters into their own hands, and attempt to bless themselves… not realizing that they control nothing.

(Vs. 8) *"Just as it is written: God has given them a spirit of stupor, eyes that they should not see, and ears that they should not hear, to this very day."*

It means:

"As the scriptures say: God has caused the people to fall asleep. God closed their eyes so they could not see, and he closed their ears so they could not hear. This continues until now."

Having an attitude of hardness toward God is not a "take control" move. He has the ultimate plan for man, whether we agree with it or not. People think they'll get some kind of revenge. They think that he has made some kind of mistake by not blessing us in the way that he has blessed others. But once you fully put your trust in him… let him guide your life, you will begin to realize the value of those blessings that he has already provided to you. God is not a master who wants to control people like a boss, but he wants to guide us, in the way of Christ, towards himself. The only requirement is that we believe in Christ, and his sacrifice on the cross. When we do that, we make ourselves a vessel for God, allowing his Holy Spirit to come in and shine his holy light in us, in order to light the way to God for others.

What does it mean... ?

"God don't like ugly."

This statement is used when someone does a wrong to someone else, that is bad, wrong, or unfair.

It means...

that people believe that God will let something bad happen to that person for their actions. They believe it is a bible truth that somewhere, somehow, revenge will be gotten as payback for the wrong that was done. It is true, but not in the way that people think.

Romans 12:19 (KJV) says:

"Dearly beloved, avenge not yourselves, but rather give place unto wrath: for it is written, Vengeance is mine; I will repay, saith the Lord."

By the scripture, people have the misunderstanding that God will throw lightning bolts, cause a tree to fall, or make a car crash in order to get his vengeance on a person. But don't forget... we have a loving God, which is why he calls us, "Dearly beloved." The way he punishes people... in many instances, is by allowing to them punish themselves.

Most of the time, when someone has wronged another person, they've done so knowingly. So in order for that person to learn the lesson of their mistakes, God will often step back and allow them to continue to live according to their *own* will. He is not a tyrant who rules with an iron fist, but he is a fair God who guides, and teaches with a loving Spirit.

It is his great teaching that people must learn… about the concept of **reaping, and sowing**. We reap or <u>*harvest*</u> in life, whatever we sow or <u>*plant*</u> in life, or in plain English… whatever way we *choose* to live… good or bad, will have an affect on whatever *happens* to us in life… good or bad. No, <u>God don't like ugly,</u> but do you?

What does it mean… ?

"The devil sure is busy."

This statement is used when multiple bad things are happening to someone, and there seems to be no apparent reason for it.

It means:

People have the misunderstanding that the devil has the power to make trouble, or cause problems in their lives. Throughout the years, he has been given the blame for the ruin of many lives, the destruction of families, and the loss of many precious things in the lives of people.

Matthew 28:18 (KJV) says:

"And Jesus came and spake unto them, saying, All power is given unto me in heaven and in earth."

By the scripture, we can know that the devil has no power at all, in heaven or on Earth. That means that he has no means to cause anything bad to happen. But in people's traditional minds, everything bad is caused by the devil. It's *partly* true, however not in the way that people think.

Bad things that happen often begin from a series of events, or missteps that have been building over a period of time, and leading up to a bad ending result. None of us are perfect…we all make mistakes. But often those mistakes start out small, and have little affect on anything, unless they have been allowed to grow into bigger troubles. If those *little* mistakes are not caught before they have time to grow, the end result will be something bad.

So, the *idea* that the devil can cause bad things to happen is in *our own minds* when we fail to realize the *ultimate power* of Jesus Christ. We *give* the devil power by making it him who has caused the bad things to happen, when *it is really those smaller bad things* that have grown, and formed the thought of a *busy* devil in our lives. The devil is busy to us only when we don't embrace the power of Jesus Christ within us, and let him have his power over our lives, that is already given to him by God.

WHAT SHOULD I PRAY FOR?

```
Y G Z V G L Y I E S H I N D B
L I X W E T H O N S R U E P X
I R P X E Q O A C H U R C H U
M P E F S B I M X A O K N M M
A V A Z F T P R O V I S I O N
F S C S S C T C B D T I A C F
I V E I T B Q O P O S J K H Q
Z A R Z K O L S G L B I L I N
B H V S H D R T T D Z O W L E
C C S T N E R A P R V A P D R
F J Y E M O H Y Q E E O L R K
R P S A U F A W E L G N L E U
C S H S D T J T R O C K G N H
B V M I K H S Y S G Q I Q T Q
A M K B E G T C Y M O I L L H
```

BOLDNESS
CHILDREN
CHRISTIANS
CHURCH
FAMILY
HOME
LOVE
PARENTS
PASTOR
PEACE
PROVISION
SAFETY
STRENGTH
WISDOM

What does it mean… ?

"Bad things happen to good people."

Doesn't it seem that way? Why is it that a person who is constantly at the heart of trouble, causing havoc wherever they go, seem to be safe, and in many cases… prosperous… but a person who has no visible faults anywhere in their life, meet a fate that they seemingly didn't deserve? To find the answer to this, you have to know that **"good"** and **"bad"** are relative terms. The definition of *good* to one person, may be different to another. Of course, the same is also true with the definition of *bad*. However, a simple answer is found in the words of Jesus when one of the disciples addressed him as "good Master." Jesus looked at the disciple, and told him this:

Mark 10:18 (KJV)

"And Jesus said unto him, Why callest thou me good? there is none good but one, that is, God."

That means that what is perceived to be good to us, is only defined by the limitations of our human minds. A person can be loving, kind, peaceful, likeable, and giving. But no one starts out that way, and there are dark corners in everyone's past, present, or future. None of us are pure... only God.

We are not able to fathom how deep or how far the goodness of God goes, which is surely beyond any realm of our understanding. That makes *God* the *definition* of good. Since none of us is God, none of us is good. Therefore, bad things happen to good people because there are *no good people*.

What is Wisdom?

1. Luke 2:40

     _____

2. Luke 2:52

     _____

3. 1 Cor. 1:24

     _____

4. Ephesians 1:17

     _____

5. Colossians 2:3

     _____

6. James 3:15

     _____

7. James 3:17

     _____

8. Rev. 7:12

     _____

Wisdom is the principal thing; therefore get wisdom:and with all thy getting get understanding. **(Prov. 4:7)**

What does it mean… ?

"Don't play with God."

It is what people say when they think someone is only pretending to be righteous or christian. Whenever a person is thought to be not as religious, as christian, or not as righteous as they want everyone to think they are, they are said to be *"playing with God."*

In some cultures, this is the equivalent to, and carries the same weight as hypocrisy. In the Old Testament, there are the scribes and pharisees who would put on their colorful robes, and parade around the city wearing their gold or jewels for all to see. They were seen as the religious leaders of the time, yet some of them were only flaunting themselves in front of the people for show. It could be said that they were *playing with God.*

Today, many people believe that if you're playing with God, you are playing with your life, because God will get you. That notion comes directly from the bible when Jesus was teaching in the temple.

Mark 12:38-40 (KJV) says:

"And he said unto them in his doctrine, Beware of

the scribes, which love to go in long clothing, and love salutations in the marketplaces, And the chief seats in the synagogues, and the uppermost rooms at feasts: Which devour widows' houses, and for a pretence make long prayers: these shall receive greater damnation."

Today, we refer it to some people who get satisfaction out of making everyone think that they are so much more into the church than the next person. They get a mental "high" out of the praise from people because they have a position in the church. They feel above others because they are able to give more money in church, or drive a nicer car than someone else to church, or even dress better at church. Those rewards are blessings. But if you have the wrong attitude, you are only satisfying your fleshly need for attention. Still, God is not going to get you, but you will eventually … bring trouble upon yourself. For that reason, <u>don't play with God.</u>

What does it mean… ?

"If I walk into a church now, it's gonna fall down."

This is something some people say if they have not attended church in a long time. They think since they have been away for so long, it is shameful, and God will somehow punish them for it. They think that everyone who goes to that church will recognize their absence over the period of time, and they will be the center of attention when they return.

It means:

They have a guilty conscience about not going to church. People think that attending church will somehow justify everything that they've ever done wrong. They think that attending makes them good and righteous… deep down. They think God will once again forgive them for their wrongs, and they will again be in good standing with him. But the truth is… the building people attend for services is not even the church. The people *themselves* are the church. The bible says:

1 Corinthians 12:12 (KJV)

" *For as the body is one, and hath many members, and all the members of that one body, being many, are one body: so also is Christ.*"

That means that all of the different faces that we see in the building are all parts of the "body" of Christ, and come together to make what we call… the "**church.**" Traditionally, many religions refer to the actual building where services are held as the church, which is fine for them, but according to the bible, it is the people within who are Christians that define the term. Christians are those who are believers in Christ. So, the building will not fall if you go to church now, because if you are a *believer* in Christ, you are part of his body, and *you are* the church.

What does it mean… ?

"I can forgive, but I will never forget."

People say this when someone has done something to them so wrong, that they feel they can't ever lose the thought of it. Often, the very sight of that person, brings back a stream of memories of the horrific thing that was done to them like the repeat of a movie.

It means:

People think that forgiveness and forgetfulness are two separate things, but they are actually part of the same action. It is hard to truly forgive someone if the feelings that were experienced during the event, are still there in the mind. It may even take professional counseling… and time, to be able to honestly forgive and forget.

Job 9:27 (KJV) says:

"If I say, I will forget my complaint, I will leave off my heaviness, and comfort myself."

Job is speaking about the wrong that he thought God had done to him in his own life. He has realized that forgetting is an integral part of forgiving, in which both are part of the healing process. Although people have every good intention of forgiving a person, humanity has not developed the ability to simply forget all about a wrong. However, in some cases, it may be easier to do when it concerns a relative, rather than a stranger. Family takes the precedence in most instances, because it's easier to forgive a family member.

In very large, very close families, forgetting is just a matter of coming together in support of each other, including the family member who caused the problem. As an individual… like Job who had no family support, it would be harder to just let it go, unless we realize that forgiveness is for ourselves more than for the other person… so is forgetting. We have to be able to do both in order to heal within, and make ourselves better for it. We will forever go through life in anger, resentment, and hatred if we cannot find the strength to conquer the wrongful thoughts that linger in our minds.

What can the Holy Spirit can Do?

1. Acts 13:2

   _____

2. Romans 8:26

   _____

3. John 15:26

   _____

4. Acts 16:6-7

   _____

5. John 16:13

   _____

6. Acts 20:28

   _____

7. Romans 8:14

   _____

8. Ephesians 1:13

   _____

Why Pray?

Most people think that praying is just the act of asking God for things, but it is much more. Praying is actually, maintaining communication with God and is essential to us as Christians because he can direct our paths as we walk in the Holy Spirit. Staying in touch with God is like having an open line to our command center where we can ask questions, receive instructions, renew our supply of faith, restore our hope, and make requests for others and ourselves. With Jesus as our intercessor, our prayers go forth,

"For there is one God, and one mediator between God and men, the man Christ Jesus." (1 Timothy 2:5).

Sources

The Holy Bible, KJV (and other   translations).

Gibilisco, Stan -

www.sciencewriter.net

Rouse, Margaret –

www.techtarget.com

www.biblegateway.com

www.techterms.com

www.pc.net

www.bestonlinedictionary.com

About the Author

As a published writer/author and speaker with over 30 years of experience as a published author, and a loyal member of the church, Lee has helped many people to change their lives. He dives right in emotionally, and personally, when faced with helping his fellowman through a problem.

He thanks God for enabling him to share his insightful vision with others, as he invites all to travel with him on his journey toward peace, through his books, and his words.

He credits his many years of work with children for his ability to capture imaginations, and for the realization that no matter what our age, we all dream.

www.ingramcontent.com/pod-product-compliance
Lightning Source LLC
Chambersburg PA
CBHW030012040426
42337CB00012BA/744